Suzanne Kamata

A GIRLS' GUIDE TO THE ISLANDS

Suzanne Kamata is the author of the award-winning young adult novel *Gadget Girl: The Art of Being Invisible,* and the author or editor of a range of books. Originally from Michigan, she now lives in Tokushima, Japan, with her family, and teaches EFL at Tokushima University. Suzanne holds an MFA from the University of British Columbia.

First published by Gemma Open Door for Literacy in 2017.

Gemma Open Door for Literacy, Inc.
230 Commercial Street
Boston MA 02109 USA

www.gemmamedia.com

Printed in the United States of America
978-1-936846-57-3

Library of Congress Cataloging-in-Publication Data applied for

Cover by Laura Shaw Design

Map on page 98 by Buyodo.

Gemma's Open Doors provide fresh stories, new ideas, and essential resources for young people and adults as they embrace the power of reading and the written word.

Brian Bouldrey
Series Editor

GEMMA

Open Door

To Lilia, travel companion
extraordinaire.

1

How can I get out of the promise that I made to my twelve-year-old daughter, Lilia?

A few weeks ago, I invited her to go with me to Osaka. We would take in an art exhibition. The latest works of the Japanese artist Yayoi Kusama would be on display at the National Museum of Art. The show finishes at the end of March.

Kusama is famous for her polka-dotted pumpkin sculptures. I've been interested in this artist for a while. This seemed like the perfect opportunity to get to know her work better. At first, I'd been planning on going alone. Maybe I

1

could go while my twins were at school. It occurred to me, however, that Lilia was old enough to appreciate Kusama's art. Plus, if we went together, I wouldn't have to worry about hurrying back to pick her up from school. My son would be okay left alone for a few hours. My daughter is multiply disabled. She often needs help.

Of course, when I proposed this outing, Lilia was eager to go. Art! A bus trip to Osaka! Polka dots! What's not to like?! So we made plans. Now Lilia is entering spring break and the exhibit is drawing to a close. I am dreading the trip. I doubt that my daughter can keep herself entertained on the long bus ride to and from Osaka. If I go by myself, I can read, daydream, and doze. With Lilia along, I might have to chat in sign language for hours. It wouldn't be relaxing.

Also, it would be tiring. Usually, going to a big city involves a lot of walking. We'd be wandering around the museum. I'd probably have to push Lilia's wheelchair up inclines. I might even have to carry her. At the thought of physical exertion, I just want to cancel everything. I'd rather stay home. But Lilia reminds me.

"We're going to look at paintings tomorrow!" she signs.

"Um, yeah," I say. I try to think of some excuse not to go.

Well, we aren't really prepared. I was planning on showing her a film I'd bought about Kusama's life and work. Afterward, I'd imagined I would discuss it with her. I've read the artist's

3

autobiography, *Infinity Net*. I know that she made macaroni sculptures because she was afraid of food. She created phallic sculptures because she was afraid of sex. I know that due to mental illness, she has lived in a psychiatric hospital in Tokyo for the past thirty years or so. She credits her art with keeping her alive. If she did not paint, she says, she would kill herself. In other words, I've done a bit of research about the artist. I have some context. However, Lilia doesn't. Not yet. Maybe we aren't ready for this.

Then again, it was me who wanted to see the Kusama exhibit in the first place. If I don't take advantage of this chance, I'll regret it later. And how can I allow myself to be lazy? Friends and family older than me are running marathons, for Pete's sake.

On top of that, my daughter hasn't been out of the house in three days. It's partly because I'm too lazy to push her wheelchair. It's partly because Lilia is too lazy to wheel herself. Kusama, who uses a wheelchair, could be inspiring to Lilia.

Also, Kusama works with simple motifs. Lilia is an aspiring artist herself. Some paintings and drawings make my daughter twist her cheek with her thumb and forefinger. This is the Japanese sign for "difficult." But Kusama's art is easy to understand. Lilia could imitate the dots and the line drawings. She could try to glue macaroni onto mannequins. Also, like my daughter, Kusama paints in spite of various challenges.

I want Lilia to understand the many hurdles the artist has had to overcome. As a child, Kusama hallucinated. She heard the voices of flowers and animals. She grew up in a wealthy but dysfunctional family. Her mother forbade her to paint. She did it anyway. She even found a way to go to New York City. In America, she made a name for herself. If Kusama could get herself halfway around the world, we should be able to make it to a museum a couple of hours away.

2

Lately I've had to literally drag my daughter out of bed in the mornings. True, Lilia can't walk. She can't hear without her cochlear implant. Even so, she is physically capable of getting out of bed *all by herself*. She can go to the toilet, wash her face, and change her clothes.

During spring break, she has been lazy. I don't really blame her. But on the morning of our expedition, she is motivated. She rises even before I do. She composes a funky outfit. She wears a black shirt with white polka dots on top. On the bottom, she dons black-and-white striped tights. Her socks are striped with blue and yellow. *Perfect*, I think, *for a viewing of the art of Yayoi Kusama.*

Lilia prepares her Hello Kitty rucksack and a handbag. She makes sure that she has her pink wallet, paper and pen, and books to read. She's ready to go before I am.

I didn't buy bus tickets in advance, but I manage to get front-row seats. They are the most accessible seats on the bus. Thanks to the Japanese welfare system, Lilia's fare is half price. We will also be able to get into the museum for free.

When the bus arrives, Lilia hoists herself up the steps. She gets into her seat with little help. I show the driver how to collapse the wheelchair. He stows it in the belly of the bus.

There are few passengers at midmorning. The traffic flows freely. It's sunny, but a bit chilly. Out the window we can see the lush green hills of Naruto. We pass the resort hotels along the beach. We cross the bridge that spans the Naruto Strait. Underneath the bridge, enormous whirlpools form when the tides change.

Next is Awaji Island, with its many onion fields. Finally, we come upon the Akashi Bridge, which connects to Honshu, the largest island in Japan. The glittering city of Kobe sprawls along the coast. It melts into Osaka, our destination.

Once we reach Osaka Station, we approach a cab. I worry that the driver will balk at the wheelchair, but he is kind. "Take your time," he urges.

I motion Lilia into the backseat. So far, so good. Within minutes, we're pulling up to the museum. Soon we're in the lobby, preparing for a look at *The Eternity of Eternal Eternity*.

3

One might think that Kusama's works would be inappropriate for children. After all, at one time she was best known for her phallic sculptures and gay porn films. She encouraged nudity in public settings as a form of protest against war. However, most of her paintings and sculptures are, in fact, child-friendly. The artist herself wears a bright red wig and polka-dotted dresses. She seems innocent in spite of her illness. Or perhaps because of it. Much of her work is playful.

Also, children are more likely than most adults to understand a fear of macaroni. In any case, my daughter is not the youngest visitor to the exhibit. Mothers and children in strollers fill the lobby. They share the elevator with us as we descend into the underground museum.

The first gallery features a series drawn in black magic marker on white canvas. It's entitled *Love Forever*. I hear a little boy say, "*Kowai!*" ("That's scary!") Is he referring to the centipede-like figures in *Morning Waves*? Perhaps he's afraid of the repetition of eyes in *The Crowd*. At any rate, he gets it. He feels Kusama's phobia, the fear that led to the work.

The next room is white. It's filled with giant tulips dotted with large red circles. This is an experiential work entitled *With All My Love for the Tulips, I Pray Forever*. Lilia is delighted with the surreal space. She enjoys the colors and the giant tulips. I feel as if I'm in a Tim

Burton film. We take several pictures, then move on.

Next we look at *My Eternal Soul*. In this painting, many of the figures that appeared in the black-and-white series return. This time they are in vivid pinks, oranges, yellows, and blues. For a Westerner like me, these colors and images seem joyful. In Japan, where mothers hesitate to dress their children in bright clothes, such hues are unsettling.

Lilia likes the colors. She pauses before the bright paintings. She reads the somewhat baffling titles. *Fluttering Flags* applies to red banner-like images. This is fairly straightforward. However, the vibrant mood of a pink canvas covered with lushly lashed eyes, a spoon, a purse, a shoe, and women's profiles contrasts with its somber title, *Death Is Inevitable*.

My favorite paintings are the self-portraits toward the end of the exhibit. As a foreigner in Japan, I can relate to *In a Foreign Country of Blue-Eyed People*. This one recalls Kusama's years in New York in the 1960s. She was a rare Japanese artist among Americans. Red dots cover the face, suggesting disease. Or dis-ease?

Lilia is partial to *Gleaming Lights of the Souls*. This is another experiential piece. We are invited to enter a small room with mirror-covered walls. Within the walls, dots of light change colors. It gives us the feeling of being among stars or planets in outer space.

Finally, we watch a short documentary about Kusama. There are no subtitles, but Lilia can see the artist at work. She sees the assistant who eases her in and out of her chair. The assistant also helps Kusama to prepare her canvases.

"See?" I want to tell her. "We all need a hand from time to time." But I don't want to disturb her concentration. I'm silent and still, letting her take in whatever she can by herself.

On the way home, I feel pleasantly exhausted, but hopeful. The trip was not as arduous as I'd anticipated. I'm also encouraged by Kusama herself, by the fact that she's found a way to make a living—and to stay alive—through art, in spite of everything. I'm not pushing my daughter toward a career in the fine arts. As a writer, I know how tough it can be. I don't necessarily expect Lilia to become famous. She doesn't need to earn money through her drawings or paintings. However, I feel sure that having art in her life will bring her joy and satisfaction. It will enrich her and give her a means of expression.

I'm hoping that with today's expedition, I've pried the world open just a little bit wider for my daughter—and for myself. I start planning future trips in my head. Next, the two of us can go to the islands of the Inland Sea.

4

To celebrate Lilia's graduation from junior high school, she and I are taking a mother-daughter trip—this time overnight—to Naoshima, an island off the coast of Shikoku.

Naoshima was once used primarily as a site to dump industrial waste. Now it is full of art museums. One of the museums has one of Claude Monet's famous water lily paintings. Tourists come from all over the world.

Monet admired Japan, and his art is very popular here. His garden in France was designed to look like a Japanese garden. In turn, a garden modeled after the one in France has been constructed farther south in Shikoku, but the painting is on Naoshima. There are no bridges connecting Naoshima to Shikoku. The only way to get there is by ferry. If it's foggy or the waves are high, the ferry doesn't run.

I have made a reservation for us at the Benesse House Museum. Each of the ten rooms in the hotel has original artwork and a view of the Seto Inland Sea.

I've been planning for us to go by bus, taxi, and then ferry, and to be met by the hotel shuttle bus. This way, Lilia and I will be able to chat in sign language en route. I'll be able to read and relax. Unfortunately, a light drizzle is predicted for the day of our trip. Dealing with a wheelchair in the rain is never fun. Although I have never driven to the ferry port in Takamatsu before, I decide to go by car.

5

On the morning of our departure to Naoshima, I load Lilia's wheelchair and a suitcase decorated with hot air balloons into the car. We set out for Takamatsu, an hour's drive north. For most of the way, we're on the highway, flying past the forested hills of Shikoku. We pass signs warning of wandering wild boars. We go through mountain tunnels. Once in the city, I follow the directions given by the navigation system on my iPhone. I manage to get us to the ferry terminal and onto the boat. Most of the other vehicles are dump trucks. Perhaps they're loaded with industrial waste for dumping in the northwest of the island. Because there is no easy way to get Lilia up on deck, we stay in the car, in the belly of the boat. We are only vaguely aware of our progress across the sea.

"Go look," Lilia encourages.

I get out of the car and peek out a window. All I can see is water.

6

We disembark about an hour later at Miyanoura Port. Fishing boats bob gently in the harbor. An enormous red polka-dotted pumpkin created by Yayoi Kusama is in a park to the left of the visitor's center. Signs helpfully indicate directions to the 007 Museum and the various art museums. In addition to the Benesse Art Site, there are the Chichu Art Museum and the Art House Project, a group of abandoned houses in which contemporary art is now exhibited.

I inadvertently take the scenic route down narrow neighborhood streets. We follow winding mountain roads that drop off to the sea. Wisps of fog hover over the cove. The scene reminds me of

Chinese ink paintings. Luckily, there is little traffic. We see only a few random hikers and cyclists. No one honks at my slow, careful driving. I can hear Lilia snapping photos of the spectacular view in the backseat. The road descends. I spot a campsite with rows of white yurts off to our left. A guardhouse is stationed in front of the road that leads to the Art Site on the right. The guard verifies that we are indeed guests at the hotel and directs us the rest of the way.

In addition to the museum, the Art Site includes a grassy area featuring colorful sculptures of snakes and cats by internationally celebrated artists such as Karel Appel, Niki de Saint Phalle, and Dan Graham. Another Yayoi Kusama pumpkin, this one yellow, is located farther down the beach. We drive past the Terrace Restaurant, where we will dine later this evening. *Drink a Cup of Tea*, a sculpture of a blue teacup by Kazuo Katase, is balanced on a stone wall. We begin to climb again. I catch a glimpse of an overturned yellow boat on another beach in a far cove.

We finally arrive at the Benesse House Museum. It's a modern gray concrete structure designed by Tadao Ando. I unload Lilia's wheelchair, help her out of the car, and push her up the ramp to the entrance.

"Welcome!" The young woman at the reception desk is French. She is speaking English. I'd been prepared to speak Japanese, so it takes me a moment to adjust. I find out later that 40 percent of visitors to the island are from abroad. It makes perfect sense to have an international staff.

The receptionist hands over our room key. It's attached to a piece of driftwood in keeping with the natural surroundings. We follow a young Japanese woman onto the elevator. We get off on the third floor and go down a hushed, dim corridor to our room. Small children are not allowed to stay in the museum hotel, presumably because the rooms contain valuable artwork, but also perhaps because they are noisy. I guess children, as yet in a wild state, are meant to stay in the yurts on the beach.

The website also makes it quite clear that there will be no discounts for individuals with special needs. The hotel

does not have "barrier-free" accommo-
dations. Oh, well. We'll manage.

"Waaah!" Lilia exclaims as she wheels
herself into the room. The furnishings
are in blond wood. The twin beds are
covered with bright white duvets. The art
is *Stern* by Thomas Ruff, two paintings
of a starry night sky. Lilia is completely
satisfied, especially since she doesn't even
need a password to access the hotel's
Wi-Fi network. She immediately begins
texting her friends.

I sigh.

7

"Let's go check out the art," I tell Lilia.

The door is too heavy for her to open by herself. I wouldn't want to leave her alone in this room, even if she'd rather stay here texting her friends. She slowly takes a recharger out of her backpack and connects it to her iPad. She is a bit reluctant. Finally, she follows me into the corridor.

Much of the art in the museum was inspired by the geography of Naoshima and was created on-site. Richard Long's walks around on the island in 1997 were the impetus for his four works in the first gallery we enter. *Inland Sea Driftwood Circle* is just that —a circle composed of wood laid out on the floor. As far as I can tell, nothing fixes it in place. I keep an eye on Lilia's wheelchair. I have to make sure that she doesn't accidentally back into the installation. What if she knocks something out of place? I can't help wondering if the museum staff sometimes has to fix the composition. This is a land of earthquakes, after all. And don't they have to dust the wood from time to time?

Another circle, called *Full Moon Stone Circle*, is outside. Two other large circles painted in earthy tones, *River Avon Mud Circles by the Inland Sea*, dominate a white wall.

"What does this one look like to you?" I ask Lilia, gesturing at the wall.

She studies it for a moment. "Donuts."

We take in Yukinori Yanagi's *Banzai*

Corner, in which hundreds of Ultraman dolls with their hands raised are lined up in front of a mirror. We look at a painting of a swimming pool by David Hockney, and Jasper Johns's *White Alphabets*, which Lilia finds underwhelming.

"They're famous artists," I say. I tell her that Jasper Johns studied art at my alma mater, the University of South Carolina.

She leans in for a closer look. Yayoi Kusama aside, she hasn't had much exposure to modern art until now. Maybe this trip will open her mind to possibilities.

"You could probably create something like this." I point at Cy Twombly's *Untitled I*. The painting is composed of repeated squiggles,

She nods. "Yes, I could."

A long ramp leads to the first floor of the museum, where Jonathan Borofsky's *Three Chattering Men* nod their heads and say "Chatter chatter chatter chatter chatter." There is also an installation by the American artist Jennifer Bartlett of overturned yellow and black rowboats. A painting of the boats—*Yellow and Black Boats* —hangs on the wall just above. I recognize the boats that I saw earlier down on the beach.

In an adjoining room, we find another work created for this site, by Jannis Kounellis. He has rolled up driftwood, old kimonos, Japanese paper, and earthenware in lead plates. The installation is untitled, leaving it open to interpretation. I see the shape of logs and a connection to industry in the materials used, an echo of Naoshima's past. "What does this one look like to you?" I ask Lilia.

"Flowers," she signs. "Roses."

Okay, I can see that, too.

Although the galleries are for the most part wheelchair accessible, one requires steps. I take a look and report back to Lilia. "It's like white paper."

It sounds boring. She doesn't want to see for herself.

Lilia wears a bright pink sweater and orange leg braces. She loves color. Therefore, it's no surprise that her favorite painting of the day is David Hockney's *A Walk Around the Hotel Courtyard Acatlan*, which is done in the vivid pinks and oranges of Mexico.

"I want to paint something like that," she signs. "Something big."

8

Upon checking in, I had received a card entitling me to a free glass of sparkling wine in the Museum Café at four thirty p.m. After going through the museum, we still have some time till happy hour. The other attractions are not open today. I propose a visit to the park farther down the hill.

I park behind the shop and restaurants and we take a little stroll down the hill. Crows caw. Pigeons rustle in the underbrush. Several foreigners cruise by on rented bicycles. Japanese tourists seem to be in the minority. We pose for photos in front of some of the sculptures, including the yellow pumpkin.

Lilia says that she is cold and wants to go back to the hotel.

When four thirty rolls around, Lilia is once again engrossed in her iPad.

"Shall we go have a drink? Some juice?"

"You go ahead," she signs. "I'll wait here."

I picture myself sitting all alone with my glass of sparkling wine while couples chat and laugh at the surrounding tables. How sad. "No way. This is our mother-daughter trip. We're supposed to spend time together talking." Sure, we could hang out in our room until dinner, but this hotel isn't cheap. I want to take advantage of all the freebies we've been offered.

She sighs.

"Look, you can bring your iPad with you." No doubt she'll have access to Wi-Fi in the café.

We take the elevator down one floor and are shown to a table with a view of the sea. The sun is slowly sinking.

9

An elderly gentleman and the Japanese woman who'd shown us to our room earlier are tending the bar. "Would you like sparkling wine, or a mimosa?" the man asks. "A mimosa is a mix of sparkling wine and orange juice."

"I'll have a glass of wine," I say, although he seems most enthusiastic about the mixed drink, "and orange juice for my daughter."

The white-haired gentleman deposits our beverages in front of us and shows me a photo of the sunset on his smartphone.

"Do you take a photo every day?" I ask him.

"Yes," he says. "Today the sun will set at six twenty p.m."

I ask if he was born here on Naoshima.

"Yes." But like most young people, he left the island after finishing school. Back in the day, there were a hundred kids in his elementary school class. Now there are about twenty. Naoshima has a junior high school, but local kids have to go to Takamatsu for high school. "I lived in Yokohama for forty years, and then I came back," he says.

The woman tells me that she is originally from Kyoto.

"Does your daughter like art?" she asks.

"Yes." I try to get Lilia to show the young woman some of the manga-style drawings that she has done on her iPad, but she shakes her head. I explain to the woman that we live in Tokushima.

I glance around the café. The other tables are mostly occupied by Westerners. From their accents, I'm guessing they're Americans and Germans. There is one Japanese couple.

By now my "one free drink" is gone, but the white-haired gentleman brings me a mimosa, unbidden. He gives Lilia another orange juice. Talk about Japanese hospitality.

10

Later, we freshen up and change our
clothes. Lilia debuts a dark purple chif-
fon dress. She adorns her wrist with her
Eiffel Tower charm bracelet. After viewing the brightly painted sculptures in
the park, I'm thinking Lilia's orange leg
braces are so Niki de Saint Phalle. And
me? I go for a slinky sleeveless black dress
and huge fake pearls.

After the drinks, I'm glad there's a
hotel shuttle to the seaside French restaurant. I wouldn't be able to manage the
twisty drive in the dark. The van lets us
out at the back entrance of the Benesse
House Park Building. A woman leads
Lilia and me to an elevator. She reaches
inside and pushes a button. We get off

on the first floor, finding ourselves in a dark, empty corridor. The receptionist had given me a map and shown me how to get to the restaurant. That was three hours and two glasses of sparkling wine ago. I forgot to bring the map. Now I'm a tad confused. I open one door, which leads to a lounge. Nope, not here. I push through the door that takes us outside and reorient myself. We go down a hallway, past the spa, past the gift shop, and arrive at the Umi no Hoshi (Stars of the Sea) restaurant. We're just in time for our six p.m. reservation.

A friendly Japanese waiter seats us at a table next to a window that looks out onto the sea through the black pines.

"Naoshima is great," Lilia signs.

"It is very nice here," I agree.

The waiter brings our first course, an amuse-bouche consisting of a micro-salad and fish mousse. Lilia takes a photo of the food.

She photographs the bread and the olive oil, pressed from the olives of Shodoshima, another small island nearby. She takes a picture of the fish. Lilia's piece has been thoughtfully cut into bite-sized pieces. When I point this out to her, she is visibly moved.

The waiter comes by with the bread basket, and Lilia takes another piece.

"Will the meat be tough?" she asks, thinking of the next course.

I realize that she is worried about using the silverware to cut her own beef. Although she has had practice cutting meat at home and during school restaurant outings, she finds it a bit of a nuisance. "They'll probably cut that for you, too."

She's glad that people are willing to help her, but she tells me that she is worried about the future. "Is there some work that I can do by myself? Will I always need help?"

In junior high school, she couldn't do an internship at the bakery because of her wheelchair. To maneuver around, she would have to touch the chair. It's supposedly dirty, according to the people in charge. When preparing food, hygiene is especially important. I can't help thinking that, with a few adaptions, she would be able to bake bread while maintaining health standards. Nevertheless, her one-day junior high school internship was at one of the welfare-supported work centers. She completed menial tasks. I'm hoping that she will have the chance to try work that is more interesting and challenging in high school. She says that she wants to do work that is related to art. To me, this seems possible.

"You'll find something that you can do," I tell her. Even if her work isn't directly related to art, she can still paint and draw. She can create sculptures and installations. Maybe we can work on something together someday. I can write the words, and she can produce the illustrations.

By the time our beef arrives, the sun has gone down. The beach beyond is cloaked in total darkness. I can't even see the stars over the sea. As I predicted, the meat has been discreetly cut. Lilia will not have to grapple with the fork and knife. She takes a picture of her plate. Each morsel is tender enough to melt in our mouths.

Dessert is chocolate soup and ice cream for me, and strawberry soup and ice cream for her. It's beautiful and delicious. Lilia takes a photo, devours her dessert, and then waits impatiently for me to sip my after-dinner coffee.

Back in our hotel room, Lilia starts to grab for her iPad.

"Let's take another look at the art," I say.

One of the perks of staying in the Museum Hotel is the privilege of visiting the galleries after hours. We have until eleven p.m.

At night, the *Chattering Men* are silent. The docents are gone. We could touch the art, and no one would know. Of course, we don't. Lilia could get out of her wheelchair, crawl up the steps, and enter the inaccessible gallery to see the all-white paintings. No one would notice. But she doesn't.

The lighting is different at night. Jennifer Bartlett's yellow and black boats are reflected in the glass window on the opposite wall. Kan Yasuda's stone sculpture glows dimly in the moonlight. The blinking neon words of Bruce Nauman's *100 Live and Die* are kind of spooky in the dark: "Laugh and Die." "Cry and Live." "Eat and Die."

At night, the museum is silent and we sleep.

11

In the morning, our view of the sea is obscured by fog. We learn that the ferries aren't running due to poor visibility. I feel a little nervous about driving on the twisty mountain roads without guardrails in the fog, and hope it will dissipate by the time we've finished our breakfast.

We go down the ramp to the first floor of the museum. The Issen Restaurant is just past the colorful David Hockney painting that Lilia likes. Inside, we are seated near the window. I have a great view of Andy Warhol's *Flowers*.

"I don't think Daddy would like it here," I muse as I spread apricot jam on my croissant.

"Why not?"

"Well, for one thing, there are no golf courses," I tell her. "Also, Daddy doesn't really like to look at art." When we'd first started dating, we had gone to some art exhibits at the Prefectural Museum in Tokushima City. Once he sat down on a bench and fell asleep in the gallery. Granted, he was hungover that day, but after we were married, he stopped going to art museums with me.

Lilia nods, thoughtfully. "Some people like looking at art, and some people don't."

An older Japanese woman dressed ostentatiously in a flowing red tunic and red leggings comes into the restaurant. She wears a scowl. She ducks her head into the kitchen to make some demand.

I think she must be from the big city, or maybe she's a famous artist. Later, I see the museum staff fussing around her and herding her into a private car.

After breakfast I tell the receptionist that we're going to the Chichu Museum. "Could you let them know that we have a wheelchair?"

Visibility is a bit better now, and I realize that we'd come in a roundabout way the day before. The Chichu Museum, just down the hill, soon comes into view. This building was also designed by Tadao Ando. It houses five paintings from Claude Monet's *Water Lily* series.

Although there is no discount for visitors with disabilities, kids aged fifteen and under are admitted for free. I'm the only one who needs a ticket.

When we arrive, a staff member is waiting to let us in. She lifts the chain blocking the rear entrance. I drive up the hill. A young woman in a white blouse and navy culottes meets us at the top and ushers us inside.

The museum is built into the mountain, like a bunker, and is lit by natural lighting. The walls are gray concrete. Most of the staff is dressed in what look like white lab coats. The brochure advises us to "maintain a quiet environment in the museum." It's like a hospital, or a church, but with a sci-fi vibe.

We are mainly here to see the Monet, so we make that our first order of business. We descend an elevator to a dark hall in which there is a rack of slippers.

"Please change your shoes," the docent says.

She has prepared wheel covers for Lilia's wheelchair tires, but they don't seem to fit. She gets a cloth and thoroughly wipes the tires. Finally, we are ready to enter the hallowed space.

The walls are blindingly white, the better to offset the deep blues and purples of Monet's sun-dappled pond. No one speaks. Lilia spends several seconds before each panel—*Water Lilies, Cluster of Grass*; *Water Lilies, Reflections of Weeping Willows*; *Water Lily Pond*.

The Chichu Museum houses work by only three artists—four, if you include the architect, Ando. The second exhibit that we visit is *Open Field* by James

Turrell. Although we have only traveled a short way down the hall, the docents wipe Lilia's wheelchair tires again as we wait in line. Only eight people are permitted into the space at a time. While we are waiting, a docent greets Lilia using sign language.

She looks at me and smiles.

I leave my shoes in a different shoe rack and enter in stocking feet. Visitors are invited to walk up a set of stairs to enter a room lit by fluorescent light. For the full effect, one must enter the room, but there is no wheelchair ramp. Turrell obviously wasn't thinking about accessibility when he designed this piece. It wouldn't have required much.

Lilia and I look up into the space from the bottom as the others mount the steps. They look like they are about to enter a spaceship, or are maybe on their way to some ritual of worship. They look like cult members.

"Do you want me to help you up the stairs?" I ask Lilia.

"No," she signs. "But you go ahead."

"No, I'll wait here with you."

"Go, go."

"Well, okay." I walk up the steps and enter the blue-lit space. It's discomfiting, surreal. A tall Western woman nearby, who seems to be here alone, gasps with joy or admiration or awe. I'm not sure what this all means, but when I go back down the steps and rejoin Lilia, I feel somewhat relieved.

12

The final exhibit, which also involves stairs, is *Time/Timeless/No Time* by Walter De Maria. Once again, Lilia urges me to go up the stairs while she waits below, regarding the large black sphere at the center of it all. The wooden sculptures are covered with gold leaf and suggest the roman numerals of a clock. Light comes in through a window on the ceiling. On sunny days, the gold must be dazzling.

"Ready for cake?" I ask Lilia when I've returned to her. It hasn't been that long since breakfast, but I thought it would be nice to try the desserts made according to Monet's own recipes, which are sold in the Chichu Café.

Lilia nods.

She pulls up to the long, blond wooden table facing the sea, which is still shrouded in mist. There are some books on hand, including a picture book about Monet, which I grab for Lilia to read while I get our food. I order a madeleine for myself, and vanilla ice cream for Lilia.

"His wife died when she was only thirty," Lilia tells me.

"Oh, yeah?" To tell the truth, I don't know all that much about Monet's personal life. I know that his wife was named Camille. She was the subject of several of his most famous paintings, including *La Japonaise*. He once hosted Blondelle Malone, an artist from Columbia, South Carolina, who traveled via Japan to meet him. I know that he had a big, bushy beard, and that he had some problems with his eyesight. Lilia quickly uncovers this fact as well.

"He had cataracts," she says, after reading a little further. Her school, the School for the Deaf, has recently combined with the School for the Blind. She has become especially sensitive to issues related to sight.

The cataracts clouding Monet's vision in both eyes caused his perception of color to change when he was in his mid-sixties. He wasn't diagnosed until 1912, when he was seventy-two. The *Water Lily* paintings in the Chichu Museum were completed over the years 1914 to 1926. In a letter to a friend, Monet wrote that "my poor eyesight makes me see everything in a complete fog. It's very beautiful all the same and it's this which I'd love to have been able to convey."

Although the water lilies in his pond at Giverny were a major theme late in his life, earlier paintings depict families eating dinner, an apple tart, a cut of meat, and preserved apricots. Monet, it seems, was a gourmand. The madeleine made according to his recipe is certainly tasty. I decide to buy a copy of a Monet recipe book in the gift shop on the way out.

While we are browsing the key rings and notepads and art books, someone knocks into something, creating a loud sound.

I catch the eye of an American guy. "Making noise is forbidden," I mock admonish.

"You're not supposed to breathe," his girlfriend adds.

We exchange smirks, and I can't help wondering what Monet would have made of this place. He'd have had to put out his cigarette and wipe the garden mud from his shoes. He wouldn't have been allowed to speak.

13

Due to the fog, the ferries still aren't running. For better or worse, we're stuck on the island. We wander around the port, where bicycles are rented for five hundred yen per day, and walk down back alleys, stumbling upon the I Love Yu (*yu* being the Japanese word for hot water) bathhouse, a veritable palace of kitsch designed by Shinro Ohtake, whose work appears in the Museum of Modern Art in New York City and the Victoria and Albert Museum in London, among other places. The outside walls are decorated with a hodgepodge of ceramic tiles and variously shaped blocks of wood. A fake penguin stands at the center of a fountain. A bubble-gum dispenser issues badges printed with the artist's name. The sixty-something couple who run the place seem unfazed by Lilia's wheelchair. The gentleman helps me heave her and her chair up the steps. Lilia crawls into the changing room.

The bottom of the bath itself is inlaid with coins and photos. A large, realistically sculpted elephant looks down on bathers from the top of the wall. Plants grow on the other side of a glass partition. It looks like a jungle. Who knew a soak in hot water could be such an adventure?

Since we'll be missing dinner, I suggest that we eat an early meal before boarding the ferry. Lilia agrees. I'm not too hungry, but we duck into a mom-and-pop place across from the ferry terminal which advertises, in magic marker on a white board, flounder in all its varieties—fried, boiled, raw. A lady in a flowered smock is eating at the back of the store. When we enter, me struggling a bit with the door and wheelchair, she comes over to help.

Lilia points to her mouth, indicating that the woman has some food on her face.

"Sorry," I say in Japanese, apologizing for my daughter's rudeness.

She shrugs it off good-naturedly and shows us to a table with a view of an amateur painting of Mount Fuji. Talk radio blares from a corner. A few other customers are also having early supper, most of them young women.

Lilia orders a bowl of udon noodles,

and I ask for curry rice and mango juice for both of us.

I look out the window and see that the fog has finally lifted.

14

"Do you want to visit Shodo Island?" I ask Lilia at the end of October. It's the largest island in the Inland Sea, home to about thirty thousand people, many of them aging. My mother-in-law went there years before on a group tour. She brought back olive oil as a souvenir. I am intrigued by the idea of a Japanese island with a Greek flavor. Because of its relatively large size and population, and its popularity with tour groups, I figure it would be somewhat accessible.

Lilia considers. I imagine the argument in her head: "Should I go to the mall with my friends? Or to a remote island with my mom?"

"We can stay overnight in a hotel," I add to sweeten the pot.

Lilia loves staying in hotels. Especially hotels with Internet access.

"Is there Wi-Fi?" she asks.

"Yes," I say. In reality, I'm not sure. Probably.

"Okay," Lilia agrees. "Let's go!"

My friend Wendy lives near Shodo Island. I ask her if she wants to join us. Lilia is very social. The more the merrier. We agree to meet at the ferry terminal. I will take my car to the island. We will all go together.

Lilia and I set out on a Saturday morning. The weather is perfect. The humidity has given way to cool breezes. We don't yet need jackets.

68

Wendy meets us at the ferry terminal. After I drive my car onto the ferry,
I park. Wendy opens the car door.

"Where are you going?" I ask.

"Up on deck." She seems surprised.

"Oh, right." I had forgotten that
most people get out of their cars during a ferry ride. The view is better on
the deck. We would be able to watch the
city shrink, and the islands grow larger.

"There's no elevator from here to the
deck," I say. "It would be hard to get
Lilia up there. We will wait in the car,
but you can go."

"I'd never thought of that," she says.
She gets back in the car.

On the island, we stop at a tourist
center for maps. "I really want to visit

the Olive Garden," I tell her. "There's a Greek windmill."

"I'll ask someone for directions," Wendy says.

I study the map while she asks the way. The island is small, so I figure we could just drive around until we find signs pointing us in the right direction. I could also use the app on my cell phone. I know, however, that Wendy likes to ask for directions.

She gets back in the car. "She said to go left and then right."

I drive through the town. Some of the streetlights are shaded by green or yellow globes. Maybe they are supposed to look like olives. They remind me of another era.

"The lights are so retro," I say.

"I don't like them," Wendy says. "They're like something from the 1960s."

The road follows the seashore. Off the coast we see fishing boats. Here and there are small clusters of olive trees. The branches are beaded with black olives. We finally come across a sign advertising the Olive Garden. I pull over and park in a handicapped parking space. A restaurant is up the hill.

"Shall we go eat lunch?" I ask.

"Yes," Lilia nods.

The hill is steep, but there are no steps. Lilia gets into her wheelchair and I begin to push her up the slope.

From the restaurant, the view of the sea is marvelous. I smell olive oil. Wendy and I order spaghetti, which comes with bread. Lilia orders Japanese noodles, which are served with tempura fried shrimp and vegetables. When the food arrives, the server tells us how to eat it.

"You should drizzle olive oil on the tempura," she says. "You should put some olive oil and herbed salt in a small dish and dip your bread in it."

According to a brochure I picked up, locals make olive lip gloss, olive soap, olive wax, olive hand cream, and olive-oil smoothies. You can even take classes in using olives to dye fabric. Every October the island holds an Olive Harvest Festival. People come to pick olives. They enter the "Healthy Olive Cooking Recipe Contest."

I imagine that the people of Shodo Island spend a lot of time thinking about new ways to use the olive oil that they produce. They seem very proud of it. The islanders have been growing olives since 1908, and from the taste of our lunch, it's clear that they have gotten quite good at it.

15

"Shall we find the Greek windmill?" I ask after we've eaten.

I had caught a glimpse of it on our way up the hill. It's actually a replica of the white windmills often seen on postcards from Mykonos. I think I know how to get there.

Wendy asks the server for directions.

"Oh, it's not here," the server says. "It's at the Shodoshima Island Olive Park."

"That's not here?"

"No, this is Olive Garden."

"Can we walk there?"

"You had better drive." She looks at the wheelchair. "Do you want me to call a man to help you go down the hill?"

Call a man? How retro! I picture a rickshaw driver or a palanquin bearer. In the past, carrying humans was work for the lower classes or even slaves. I can't bring myself to request "a man."

"That's okay," I tell the server. "We'll manage."

I back Lilia's wheelchair carefully down the hill. My thigh and arm muscles strain.

Olive Park is just down the road. According to the brochure, the chalk-white building is "an exact replica" of an ancient Greek building. The brochure continues, "You may feel as if you are standing on an island in the Aegean Sea."

I'm surrounded by people speaking

Japanese. Somehow I still feel as if I am on an island in the Inland Sea.

I really want to see the Greek wind-mill, but it's down another hill.

"I don't care if I see it," Wendy says. "I can stay here with Lilia while you go."

I ask Lilia if she wants to see the windmill.

"Yes!" she replies.

Wendy and I take turns backing the wheelchair down the hill. It's laborious, and maybe dangerous. If we lose control, we could all be injured. I'm starting to wish that we had the help of that man, whoever he is.

At last, we enter an olive grove and get close to the white windmill, which was built to commemorate the friendship between Shodo Island and Milos Island in Greece. Emperor Hirohito planted an olive tree near the windmill.

I take some photos. Lilia takes some photos. As we walk back to the main building, I pluck an olive from a branch. I pop it into my mouth. It's bitter. The skin is tough. I spit out the black skin. So much for raw olives.

We enter the small museum. A large statue of Athena greets us. Some brooms are on sale. They are imitations of brooms in a movie about Kiki, a young witch who runs a delivery service, which has recently been filmed on the island.

Lilia wants to watch the film about olive cultivation on the island. While she watches, I look at the exhibits. There

are photos of Japanese women in kimonos covered with aprons, pressing olives.

"They don't look happy," Wendy says.

"It looks like hard work," I add. "And
in those clothes!"

16

Anger at the Bottom, an art installation by Takeshi Kitano, is in another small port town called Sakate. In Japan, the artist is a famous comedian called Beat Takeshi. He's often on TV. In the West, he is considered a serious actor, writer, and artist. He created this work of art with another artist, Kenji Yanobe.

At first glance, this installation is a well. On the hour, however, a monster rises out like a jack-in-the-box. Water spews from its mouth. I think that Lilia would enjoy seeing this. She loves stories about ghosts and monsters.

"Why don't you ask someone how to get there?" Wendy suggests. An elderly man is walking by the side of the road. "Why don't you ask him?"

"But there's nowhere to pull over," I object. We can ask once we get a bit closer if we need to.

We pass a soy sauce factory, and a small gift shop advertising soy sauce–flavored ice cream. *Yuck,* I think. But Lilia signs that she wants ice cream.

"Later," I sign back, determined to see the monster rise from the well. It's almost three o'clock. If we're late, we'll have to wait another hour to see the beast rise up.

We arrive at the port. Another sculpture, which resembles a silver star, faces the harbor. Some elderly men sit idly in front of a nearby building. I decide to ask one of them where the installation is located. I show him the photo I had printed from the Internet.

"Where is this?"

He points toward some houses. People probably ask him all the time. I wonder how the locals feel about all the foreign visitors to their sleepy village.

"Is it within walking distance?"

"Yes, but there are few tourists now so you would be able to park closer." He nods at the wheelchair. "It would be better to drive."

First, I help Lilia use the bathroom. The toilet is not accessible. It's the kind that you have to squat over. I have to hold her up, which is difficult.

Meanwhile, Wendy talks to the man. When I come back, she tells me about their conversation.

"I asked him if he feels bored here."

"What did he say?"

"He said 'yes,'" Wendy replies.

Wendy says that she has to go back to Takamatsu. We decide that I will drop her off at the nearest ferry terminal and then Lilia and I will come back to see the monster. After that, we'll go farther north to our hotel.

I notice that there are many signs in English directing visitors to *Anger at the Bottom*. I didn't really need to ask how to get there. I follow the signs down a narrow road. We pass a persimmon tree heavy with fruit. There's another slight incline. I find a parking area near the well. The monster is already out of the well, but it isn't moving.

Lilia gets into her wheelchair and I begin pushing her up the hill. She could help me by gripping the wheels and moving them forward. She doesn't. She sits with her hands on her lap on top of her sketchbook.

"Go, Mama, go!" she says.

I huff and puff. "What do you mean? Why aren't you helping?"

Surprised at my reaction, she grabs on to the wheels and pulls.

At the well, the monster is still. This is the off-season. As the man at the harbor said, there aren't many tourists this time of year. Perhaps the monster doesn't rise and spit out water on the hour in this season. Maybe it stays in place.

The monster's red eyes seem to stare

at the sea. I detect a yearning in its expression. Its lips are pressed together. No teeth are visible.

The neighborhood is quiet. The only sounds are the flapping of a crow's wings and the twitter of an invisible bird. A slight breeze stirs the goldenrods.

I wait while Lilia sketches the monster. I'm disappointed that she couldn't see it in motion. Since it isn't moving, however, she takes her time drawing it.

When she finishes, she shows me her work.

"Good job," I say. "Now how about some soy sauce–flavored ice cream?"

17

I read that the sunset somewhere on Shodo Island has been rated one of Japan's hundred best sunsets. Since our hotel room has a view of the sea, I'm eager to check in before sunset so we can watch.

I drive along twisty mountain roads, past a quarry, and past stone sculptures, down to another tiny port town in a secluded cove. I check us in to the hotel.

"You can borrow DVDs," the desk clerk says. "Or borrow books."

The lounge is filled with comfortable white leather armchairs. Some books in English are on a shelf, as well as many books in Japanese. I grab a DVD of a movie called *24 Eyes*. It's based on a novel written by Sakae Tsuboi, a famous Japanese writer who was born in Shodoshima.

Our room is on the eighth floor. Although we can look out upon the sea from the bathtub, I discover that a mountain is blocking our view of the sunset.

"There's no Wi-Fi!" Lilia signs in a panic. She holds her iPad up as proof.

"You can use the Internet downstairs in the lobby." I'm secretly happy that she won't be able to text in the room. We can concentrate on the movie. Lilia wants to go to the *24 Eyes* Movie Village the next day. If we don't watch it beforehand, we won't appreciate the theme park.

She is grumpy until it's time to go downstairs.

We have dinner in the restaurant on the first floor. All the food is fresh and healthy. We eat fish. Dessert is peeled grapes and slices of persimmon. Afterward, Lilia texts with her friends and her father for a little while in the lobby. I sit in one of the cushy armchairs and read.

After a while, we go back to our room and watch the movie.

The story of *24 Eyes* is about a young teacher from the larger island of Shikoku who gets a job on Shodo Island. It begins in the 1920s. Most people on Shodo Island were poor. They wore kimonos. The teacher wears Western clothes and rides a bicycle, which shocks everyone on the island. Later, of course, everyone grows to love the teacher.

In the movie, there is a lot of singing. The children sing about dragonflies and crows. There is also a lot of crying. One girl has to give up her dream of going to music school because her parents are against it. One girl gets sick and dies. Three boys go off to war. Many miserable things happen. Sometimes there is singing and crying at the same time. Lilia cries, too. I bring her tissues and give her a hug.

18

The Movie Village is on the southern coast of the island. At one point, the curvy seaside road narrows. A man dressed in uniform motions for me to stop.

I lower my window. "Yes?"

"There are two big tour buses coming," he says. "Drive carefully."

How considerate! I drive slowly. When the two buses come, I pull over to the side of the road as far as I can. They whoosh past.

At the Movie Village, I discover that Shodo Island is a popular location for filmmakers. It occurs to me that the locals maintain the nostalgic feel of the island on purpose. This is the perfect place to make a movie set in the past.

Many of the tourists at the theme park are much older than us. I spot a group of senior citizens communicating in sign language. One of them notices that I am signing to Lilia. The woman approaches us.

"Where are you from?" she asks in sign language.

"Tokushima," Lilia signs back.

The woman signs that she is from Osaka.

"Is that your mother?" She gestures to me.

I'm pleased. We look nothing alike. When we are in America, most people think she is adopted.

"Yes," Lilia replies. She draws her hand down the middle of her face. "I am half."

"It's the first time I've met an American," the woman signs.

19

We look at the old-fashioned wooden buildings. Kimonos are hung on bamboo poles, as if someone has just finished the laundry. Shops sell vintage toys and candies. Visitors try to walk on bamboo stilts or roll a hoop with a stick.

When I was a child, I could walk on stilts. I think I will still be able to do it.

"Here," I say, giving Lilia my phone. "Take a picture of me." I try to get up on the stilts and fail. Lilia laughs. People start to gather.

"Never mind," I say. It isn't quite like riding a bicycle. I can't do it anymore.

We come to a restaurant with painted pictures of Japanese movie stars propped in front. At the entrance is a photo of the food served. The restaurant's theme is Shōwa-era school lunch. I ate Japanese school lunches when I first came to Japan. I taught English at junior high schools, and I ate with the students. I don't feel nostalgic for those lunches, but Lilia wants to eat here.

We go inside. Posters from different movies filmed on Shodo Island cover the walls. Lilia knows of them, but I don't. Some clothes worn in one movie are on display in a corner.

We order school lunch. It's served on a metal tray, just as I remember. There is a bowl of watery curry, a big white roll sprinkled with sugar, and a tangerine. Lilia gets milk in a bottle. I ask for the milk mixed with coffee, also served in a bottle. To tell the truth, it isn't that great. I'm glad that the food in Japan has gotten better.

Lilia wants to visit the monkey park. She also wants to check out the ravine with a ropeway going across it. Sadly, we don't have enough time.

"Is it okay if we go home now?" I ask her.

"Yes," she signs. "I can come again with my friends."

At first, I'm startled by her pronouncement. I imagined taking more trips with my daughter. We'd go to Italy! To England! To France! But lately she seems to be more interested in doing things with her friends. Maybe I will lose my traveling companion.

Then again, maybe that's okay. I want for her to be independent. I want her to have a rich life, even without me. Now that she knows this island is here, she can return. She can visit Naoshima and Osaka and lots of other places with her friends. And yes, sometimes with me.

We drive along the coast, back to the ferry port. The sea glistens in the late afternoon sun. Sometimes it seems as if all the beauty of the world is within our reach.

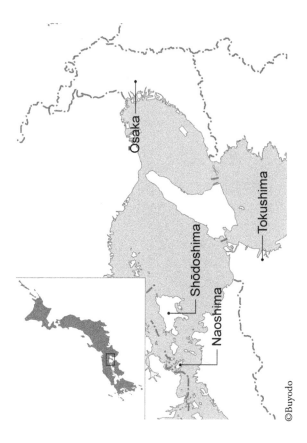

Ōsaka

Tokushima

Shōdoshima

Naoshima

©Buyodo

VOCABULARY LIST

accessible: easy to enter or easy to use for all people, despite their disabilities

amuse-bouche: French expression ("amuse mouth") that means an appetizer

barrier-free: accessible to people of all abilities, such as those who use wheelchairs

cochlear implant: a device that sends electronic signals to the brain where they are interpreted as sound. Cochlear implants allow people who are deaf to experience sound.

discomfiting: making one feel uncomfortable

docents: museum guides who supervise the galleries. Docents are often volunteers.

gourmand: a person who enjoys fine food

installation: a work of art that is created or constructed on the site where it is exhibited

kitsch: in poor taste, but with a playful feel; low brow art often made with images from pop culture

manga: Japanese-style comics, often featuring characters with big eyes.

palanquin: a covered chair on four poles, carried on the shoulders of men. These were formerly used in East Asia to carry aristocrats.

phobia: an extreme or irrational fear

udon: thick white noodles made of flour popular in Japan, usually served in broth. Takamatsu Prefecture is famous for its udon.

surreal: an artistic style that has the quality of a dream or a fantasy

yurt: a circular Mongolian-style tent

CPSIA information can be obtained
at www.ICGtesting.com
Printed in the USA
LVHW111915170921
698109LV00001B/56

9 781936 846573